Vocabulary Tales™

One of a Kind!

by Liza Charlesworth
illustrated by Amy Wummer

SCHOLASTIC INC.
New York • Toronto • London • Auckland • Sydney
Mexico City • New Delhi • Hong Kong • Buenos Aires

Designed by Maria Lilja
ISBN-13: 978-0-545-08703-2 • ISBN-10: 0-545-08703-1

First printing, October 2008

12 11 10 9 8 7 6 5 4 3 2 1   8 9 10 11 12 13/0

Building Vocabulary With This Book

This book contains eight key words that are important for all children to know. Read the story straight through for enjoyment. Then read it again, pausing to define and discuss each key word. Follow-up the tale with the fun activities on pages 14–16. When you're done, celebrate—kids will have added eight great words to their vocabularies!

I'm Henry Justin Bartlebee—
also known as me, me, me!

KEY WORD: extraordinary

Simple Definition: extra special

Sample Sentence: Wow, that painting you made was quite *extraordinary*!

I'm **extraordinary**! I'm one of a kind!
I'm a superhero! (Well, in my own mind.)

I can run really fast. I can jump really high.
I can write my whole name and eat a whole pie!

KEY WORD: **proud**

Simple Definition: feeling good about what you have done

Sample Sentence: Stella was *proud* to be able to ride her bike without training wheels.

I can hang upside down while I play the kazoo.
This makes me feel happy and very **proud**, too.

KEY WORD: **emotions**

Simple Definition: strong feelings

Sample Sentence: Theo had many different *emotions* about starting first grade.

I have lots of **emotions**. I'm happy. I'm sad.
I'm scared and I'm silly and, sometimes, I'm mad.

KEY WORD: curious

Simple Definition: to want to find out more about something

Sample Sentence: Julia was *curious* to learn more about Pilgrims, so she read three books about them.

I'm **curious**, too. I need to know more about all those giant dinosaurs.

KEY WORD: independent

Simple Definition: able to do things all by yourself

Sample Sentence: It made Jack feel very *independent* to ride his bike over to Jill's house all by himself.

I'm quite **independent**. I tie my own shoe. I take my own shower. I even shampoo!

I walk my dog. His name is Mickey.
When he licks my face, it feels really sticky!

KEY WORD: imagine

Simple Definition: to pretend

Sample Sentence: Amber likes to put on a sparkly gown and *imagine* that she is a princess.

I like to **imagine**. Pretending is great.
Look! I'm a frog. Now, I'm a snake.

KEY WORD: patient

Simple Definition: able to wait without getting upset

Sample Sentence: Teddy was *patient* and waited until his party was over to open all his presents.

I like to read. I like to learn.
I try to be **patient** and wait for my turn.

I love to draw with a marking pen.
When I make a mistake, I just try again.

KEY WORD: perfect

Simple Definition: without any mistakes

Sample Sentence: Megan thought her grandma's yummy chocolate-chip cookies were *perfect*.

I don't need to be **perfect**. I just need to be me—
The very best person this Henry can be!

Meaning Match

all-about-me words

Listen to the definition. Then go to the WORD CHEST and find a vocabulary word that matches it.

1. strong feelings
2. without any mistakes
3. to want to find out more about something
4. feeling good about what you have done
5. able to do things all by yourself
6. extra special
7. able to wait without getting upset
8. to pretend

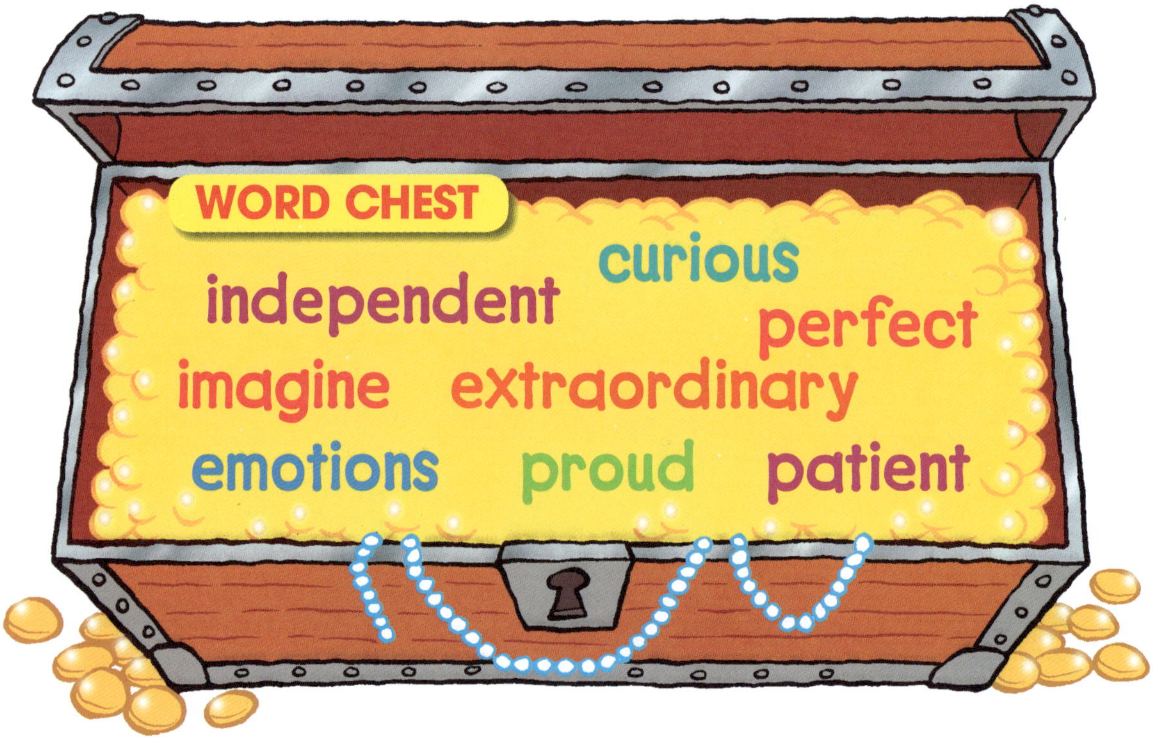

Answers: 1. emotions 2. perfect 3. curious 4. proud 5. independent 6. extraordinary 7. patient 8. imagine

Vocabulary Fill-ins

all-about-me words

Listen to the sentence. Then go to the WORD BOX and find the best word to fill in the blank.

WORD BOX

patient	proud	independent	emotions
curious	imagine	extraordinary	perfect

1 Laura was so __________ to find out who her first-grade teacher would be.

2 My grandpa is super special. He is an __________ man!

3 James loves to __________ that he is a cowboy in the Wild West.

4 Jenna felt excited, happy, and worried. She had many __________.

5 Doug stood in the long line without complaining. He was very __________.

6 Keisha felt so __________ when she scored the winning soccer goal.

7 Megan does her homework without any help. She is very __________.

8 Henry Justin Bartlebee wrote his name without any mistakes. It was __________!

Answers: 1. curious 2. extraordinary 3. imagine 4. emotions 5. patient 6. proud 7. independent 8. perfect

Vocabulary Questions

all-about-me words

Listen to the question. Think about it. Then answer.

1. What animal are you **curious** to learn more about?
2. What is your favorite thing to **imagine** in your mind?
3. Describe an **extraordinary** day you had. What did you do?
4. What is your **perfect** meal? Describe it.
5. Can you remember a time you had to be **patient**? Tell about it.
6. What makes you feel **independent**?
7. How many **emotions** can you name? Make a list.
8. Think about all the things you can do. Which one makes you the most **proud**?

Extra: Can you think of some more all-about-me words? Make a list.